NBA's TOP 10
COMEBACKS

BY BRIAN HOWELL

10 9 8 7 6 5 4 3 2 1

NBA's
TOP 10

SportsZone

An Imprint of Abdo Publishing
abdopublishing.com

abdopublishing.com

Published by Abdo Publishing, a division of ABDO, PO Box 398166, Minneapolis, Minnesota 55439. Copyright © 2019 by Abdo Consulting Group, Inc. International copyrights reserved in all countries. No part of this book may be reproduced in any form without written permission from the publisher. SportsZone™ is a trademark and logo of Abdo Publishing.

Printed in the United States of America, North Mankato, Minnesota
042018
092018

THIS BOOK CONTAINS
RECYCLED MATERIALS

Cover Photo: Marcio Jose Sanchez/AP Images
Interior Photos: Eric Gay/AP Images, 4–5, 8–9; L. M. Otero/AP Images, 7; Focus On Sport/ Getty Images Sport/Getty Images, 11; Michael Conroy/AP Images, 12; Darron Cummings/AP Images, 13; Warren M. Winterbottom/AP Images, 15; Charles Rex Arbogast/AP images, 16, 17; Winslow Townson/AP Images, 18; Mark Avery/AP Images, 19; Robert Kaiser/AP Images, 20–21; Tim DeFrisco/Allsport/Getty Images Sport/Getty Images, 21; Zoran Milich/Allsport/ Getty Images Sport/Getty Images, 22–23; John W. McDonough/Sports Illustrated/Getty Images, 23; Ron Schwane/AP Images, 24–25; Eric Risberg/AP Images, 26; Ken Blaze/USA Today Sports/Newscom, 27

Editor: Bradley Cole
Series Designer: Craig Hinton

Library of Congress Control Number: 2017962509

Library of Congress Cataloging-in-Publication Data

Names: Howell, Brian, author.
Title: NBA's top 10 comebacks / by Brian Howell
Other titles: NBA's top ten comebacks
Description: Minneapolis, Minnesota : Abdo Publishing, 2019. | Series: NBA's top 10 |
      Includes online resources and index.
Identifiers: ISBN 9781532114496 (lib.bdg.) | ISBN 9781532154324 (ebook)
Subjects: LCSH: Comebacks--Juvenile literature. | Basketball--Records--United States--
      Juvenile literature. | Basketball--History--Juvenile literature. | National Basketball
      Association--Juvenile literature.
Classification: DDC 796.323--dc23

TABLE OF
CONTENTS

INTRODUCTION

It was Game 1 of the 2017 Western Conference finals, and Stephen Curry and the Golden State Warriors were buried. The San Antonio Spurs led by 25 points in the second quarter. The Spurs seemed sure to win at that point. But Curry and the Warriors got hot. Golden State came back to win 113–111.

There's a lot about sports that makes them great, including superstar players and amazing plays. It's hard to top a thrilling comeback, though. Throughout National Basketball Association (NBA) history, there have been dozens of amazing comebacks.

A great comeback happens when a team looks completely defeated, and then finds a way to win. It can be rallying from a huge deficit, as Curry and the Warriors did. Other times, a great comeback happens in the final seconds of a game. Then there are the comebacks when a team is about to be eliminated from the playoffs, only to rally and win the series.

SOUTHWEST
Frost
Frost
TEXAS LOTTERY
TEXAS LOTTERY
SPURS
12
30
SPURS

10

Reggie Miller (31) sinks a three-point shot against New York.

MILLER LEADS PACERS

All the New York Knicks had to do was hang on for 18.7 seconds. It was Game 1 of the Eastern Conference semifinals on May 7, 1995. The Knicks were playing at home in Madison Square Garden. With time winding down, they held a 105–99 lead over the Indiana Pacers.

Unfortunately for the Knicks, shooting guard Reggie Miller was on the other team. With 16.4 seconds left, Miller hit a three-pointer. This wasn't a surprise. Miller was one of the greatest three-point shooters in NBA history. His shot cut New York's lead to 105–102. It was only the beginning.

Miller stole the inbounds pass. Inside the three-point arc, he turned and took a couple of steps back. He drilled another three-pointer to tie the game with 13.2 seconds left. Those two shots changed the game.

Moments later, the Knicks had multiple chances to regain the lead. John Starks took two free throws. He missed both. Then Knicks star Patrick Ewing got the rebound and missed a shot from 10 feet.

Miller grabbed Ewing's rebound and was fouled. With 7.5 seconds left on the clock, he hit two free throws to give Indiana the winning points. He delivered a remarkable comeback victory for the Pacers.

Miller finished with 31 points. The last eight were the dagger to the Knicks' heart, though. The Pacers won the series four games to three. But they needed a miracle in Game 1, and Miller provided it.

SHARPSHOOTER

Reggie Miller played his entire 18-year career with the Indiana Pacers. In that time, he was one of the league's best shooters. He made 2,560 three-pointers in his career. At the time of his retirement, that was an NBA record.

Dwyane Wade and the Heat came back from the brink against Dallas in the NBA Finals.

CRANKING UP THE HEAT

In the 2006 NBA Finals, the Dallas Mavericks were making it look easy. Seeking their first championship, the Mavericks defeated the Miami Heat by 10 points in Game 1. In Game 2, they won by 14.

In Game 3, Dallas led by 13 points with 6:34 to play. If they held on, Dallas would have had a 3–0 lead in the series. No NBA team has ever come back from a 3–0 deficit to win a playoff series.

Wade was asked what was his mindset as the deficit grew. "At that moment, looking up at the score thinking, 'No, I ain't going out like this,'" Wade said.

During the next two minutes, Wade scored five straight points to spark the rally. Wade, in fact, scored 12 of his game-high 42 points in the last 6:30. The Heat outscored the Mavericks 22–7 down the stretch to win 98–96. Dallas never recovered.

Miami won Game 4 by 24 points to tie the series. Then they won Game 5 in overtime and won Game 6 by three points. Wade averaged 39.3 points in the last four games and won Most Valuable Player (MVP) honors.

By winning four games in a row, the Heat stunned the Mavericks and claimed their first NBA championship.

08

BUCKS DOWN HAWKS

When the Milwaukee Bucks played the Atlanta Hawks on November 25, 1977, there was no championship on the line. The game was simply an early-season contest between two good teams. History was made at Atlanta's Omni Coliseum that night, however.

For most of the game, the Hawks appeared to be on their way to an easy win. They jumped to a 35–22 lead after one quarter. Going into the fourth quarter, Atlanta's lead had grown to 104–76.

With 8:43 left, Atlanta led by 29 points, 111–82. No team in the NBA had ever lost that big a fourth-quarter lead. On that night, however, the Bucks stunned the Hawks. Over the last 8:43 of the game, the Bucks outscored the Hawks 35–4. That gave them a remarkable 117–115 victory.

Led by star small forward Junior Bridgeman, Milwaukee put together the largest fourth-quarter comeback ever in the NBA. Bridgeman could tell the Hawks thought the game was over when they had a big lead. "It seems they lost their fight," he said after the game.

Bridgeman led the Bucks with 24 points, 16 of them in the fourth quarter. He was one of several players who hit big shots during the comeback. With 27 seconds left in the game, point guard Lloyd Walton drilled a shot to tie the game at 115–115.

Marques Johnson dunks the ball with one hand.

Moments later, Bucks forward Marques Johnson drove toward the hoop, but he was fouled. Johnson went to the line and buried two free throws in the closing seconds. Those were the winning points in a remarkable comeback.

There are no video highlights of that game. And by season's end, neither team was among the best in the league. Still, that night became one of the most memorable in NBA history.

07

LeBron James scores against the Pacers in the 2017 playoffs.

CAVS STUN PACERS

Throughout his career, LeBron James has done a lot of amazing things on the court. So, it should not have come as a surprise that on the night of April 20, 2017, James sparked one of the greatest comebacks in NBA history.

James and the Cleveland Cavaliers were playing the Indiana Pacers in the first round of the Eastern Conference playoffs. It was Game 3. The Cavaliers won the first two, but fueled by the energy of their fans, the Pacers were dominant early. By halftime, they had built a 25-point lead over the Cavaliers. No team in NBA playoffs history had ever come back from that large a halftime deficit. Leave it to James to change history.

Kevin Love (0) attempts to guard Indiana's Myles Turner.

"The only thing that matters is a win—that's what I'm here for," James said. That's exactly what he and the Cavs did. Just 22 seconds into the third quarter, J. R. Smith drained a three-pointer. That sparked a 13–3 run to start the second half and sliced the deficit to 15. They never looked back from there. In the second half, the Cavs outscored the Pacers by 30 points to win 119–114. James dominated all aspects of the game. He had a triple-double, with 41 points, 13 rebounds, and 12 assists. He scored 28 of his points in the second half.

The comeback victory gave Cleveland a 3–0 lead in the best-of-seven series. "To win on the road in the postseason is already tough enough," James said. "For us to win in the fashion we did tonight is even tougher. As a group, we don't take that for granted."

Three nights later, the Cavs finished the sweep with a 106–102 victory. That Game 3 comeback will be the win that fans remember the most.

06

Paul Hoffman (32) shoots the basketball overhead against Philadelphia.

BULLETS FLY PAST WARRIORS

Before LeBron James and the Cleveland Cavaliers came back by 25 points in a 2017 playoff game, the Baltimore Bullets held the record for the previous biggest comeback. Perhaps the most impressive part was that the record had stood for 69 years.

Prior to the Cavs' comeback, the largest halftime deficit overcome in NBA playoff history was 21 points. That comeback was pulled off by the Baltimore Bullets on April 13, 1948. It was Game 2 of the NBA Finals. There was no three-point shot or shot clock at that time. That made coming back from a 21-point deficit even more difficult.

After losing Game 1, Baltimore was in danger of falling to 0–2 in the series. The Philadelphia Warriors took a 41–20 halftime lead. "In those days, if you got behind that far, the game was over," Baltimore's Buddy Jeannette said. "But somehow we did. We took our time and made our shots and caught [them]. I don't know if we were so good or Philly was so bad."

By the end of the third quarter, the Bullets had cut the Warriors' lead to 48–40. The Bullets kept the momentum in the fourth quarter to steal the win. Connie Simmons led the Bullets with 25 points as they shocked the Warriors with a 66–63 victory in Game 2 of the Finals.

HERE AND GONE

The Baltimore Bullets won the NBA championship in 1948, their first season. But that title didn't launch a dynasty. In fact, the Bullets played just six more seasons. In 1954, the team disbanded.

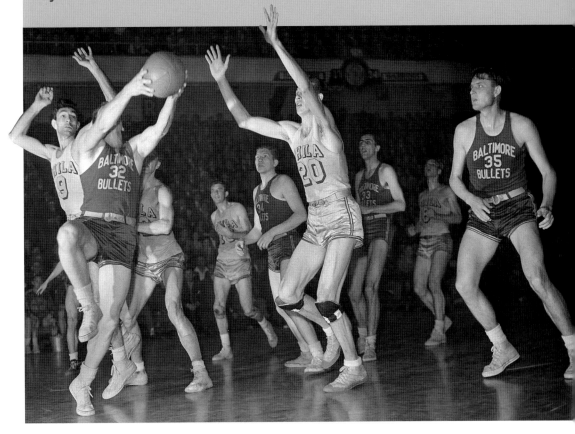

The Bullets won the next two games as well. Then in Game 6, they rolled to an 88–73 victory to take the series, four games to two. It was the only championship the Bullets ever won, and it never would have happened without that thrilling comeback in Game 2.

KINGS WITH ROYAL FINISH

On December 21, 2009, the Chicago Bulls built a 35-point lead against the visiting Sacramento Kings. For two and a half quarters, everything went right for the Bulls. With 8:50 to play in the third quarter, Chicago led 79–44.

Chicago had been in control of the game all night. But after a jumper by John Salmons gave the Bulls their largest lead, they suffered a letdown. The Bulls relaxed while the Kings stole the momentum. The final 21 minutes belonged to the Kings. Rookie Tyreke Evans drove to the hoop for a layup that sparked the comeback.

The Kings dominated the rest of the way. Sacramento finished the third quarter on a 19–5 run to pull within 19 points.

Tyreke Evans, right, fights off Joakim Noah for a loose ball.

The Kings outscored the Bulls by 39 in the final 21 minutes. Sacramento pulled off the comeback, 102–98. Through the 2016–17 season, it was the second-largest comeback in league history.

Then they got an unexpected contribution from an unlikely hero. In the first three quarters, little-used forward Ime Udoka had just two points. Then he scored 15 points early in the fourth quarter to help the Kings pull within 95–91 with 2:28 to play.

Evans took over for the Kings at that point. He outscored the Bulls by himself 9–3 down the stretch. His long jump shot with 50 seconds left gave the Kings a 99–96 lead. Evans finished with 23 points and eight rebounds to lead the Kings, who outscored the Bulls by 39 in the final 21 minutes. The Kings pulled off the comeback, 102-98. Through the 2016–17 season, it was the second-largest comeback in league history.

04

Sasha Vujacic shoots a three-pointer against Boston in the 2008 NBA Finals.

CELTICS RALLY PAST RIVALS

Since the NBA began in the 1940s, two teams traditionally have dominated. Those two teams, the Boston Celtics and the Los Angeles Lakers, met in the 2008 NBA Finals.

Boston jumped out to a 2–1 lead. Game 4 was on June 12, 2008. The Lakers got off to a fast start as they looked to even the series. When Sasha Vujacic hit a three-pointer midway through the second quarter, the Lakers' lead increased to 24 points, 45–21. No team ever had rallied from that big a deficit in NBA Finals history.

The Celtics tried to come back, but they were still down by 20 midway through the third quarter. Then, led by stars Ray Allen and Paul Pierce,

Kobe Bryant (right) guards Paul Pierce during the 2008 NBA Finals.

18

LAKERS VS. CELTICS

Through the 2016–17 season, the Los Angeles Lakers and Boston Celtics had met in the NBA Finals 12 times, with Boston winning nine times. From 1959–69, they played in the Finals seven times, with Boston winning each time. From 1984–87, they met three times in four seasons, with the Lakers winning twice. The Celtics won the 2008 matchup. The Lakers won their last meeting in 2010.

Boston took over. The Celtics outscored the Lakers 21–3 in the last six minutes of the third quarter. That cut their deficit to 73–71.

With 4:07 left in the fourth quarter, the Celtics finally took the lead. Eddie House made a jump shot for an 84–83 Boston lead. The Celtics never trailed again, winning the game 97–91. Pierce and Allen combined for 39 points to go up 3–1 in the series. And the Celtics went on to claim their record 17th championship.

03

Earvin Johnson drives the ball against Jerry Reynolds of the Seattle SuperSonics.

LAKERS SET A RECORD

On May 14, 1989, the Los Angeles Lakers had a 3–0 lead against the Seattle SuperSonics in the Western Conference semifinals. Going into Game 4, the Lakers were looking for the series sweep.

Playing in front of their home crowd, however, the SuperSonics came out hot. Just 14 minutes into the game, Seattle took a 29-point lead, 43–14. Nothing was going right for the Lakers. Their head coach, Pat Riley, wasn't too happy with the officiating, either. Riley was given a technical foul for arguing with the referees. The technical free throw gave Seattle a 48–21 lead.

But Riley's anger seemed to spark the Lakers, who started to play like the dominant team they had been all year. During the final 5:20 of the first half, they went on a 16–0 run. That cut the Seattle lead to 11 at halftime. That was the turning point for Los Angeles.

In the second half, Los Angeles kept the momentum going. They were sharp with their shooting. They played great

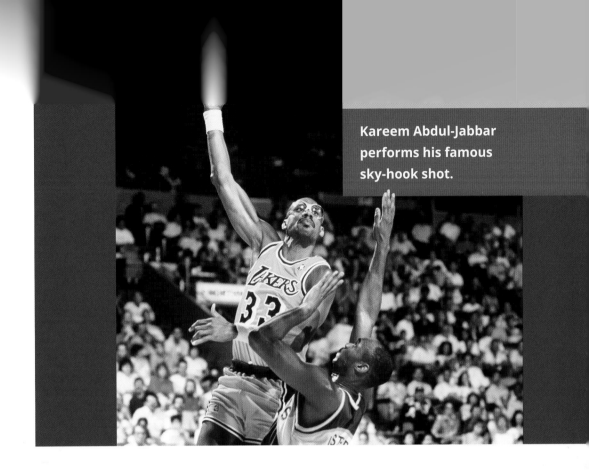

Kareem Abdul-Jabbar performs his famous sky-hook shot.

defense. Finally, with 6:14 to play in the game, the Lakers took their first lead on two free throws by Orlando Woolridge.

The game remained close from there, but Los Angeles hit important free throws down the stretch. Los Angeles stunned the Sonics for a 97–95 victory to finish the series. The 29-point deficit is the largest ever overcome in a playoff game.

"We've come back before, but not like this," Riley said. "And not in the playoffs. In the playoffs, when a team gets you down, forget it." But the Lakers never quit. James Worthy had 33 points. Johnson had 17 points, nine rebounds, and nine assists.

The Lakers probably would have won the series anyway. But their Game 4 comeback made it even more thrilling.

02

Jeff Hornacek brings the ball up court.

JAZZ TUNE OUT NUGGETS

When the Denver Nuggets traveled to Salt Lake City on November 27, 1996, not many expected them to get a win.

After all, the Nuggets were one of the worst teams in the league. The Utah Jazz, meanwhile, were one of the best teams. They would finish that season with the second-best record in the NBA.

Led by sharpshooters Bryant Stith and Dale Ellis, however, the Nuggets were looking for an upset win.

Stith drilled seven three-pointers and scored 31 points that night. Ellis kept burying shots, too, and finished with 25 points. Led by the duo, the Nuggets built a huge 36-point lead against the Jazz. It was a shock to Utah fans.

The Nuggets made 14 of their first 15 shots in the game. At halftime, Denver's lead was 34 points, 70–36.

The second half was a very different game. Denver, which seemingly couldn't miss in the

Karl Malone shoots a free throw.

first half, made just six shots in the second. The Jazz, on the other hand, got hot.

Forward Karl Malone put his power on display. He had 31 points and 17 rebounds, dominating near the basket. Jeff Hornacek did his part by hitting jumper after jumper. He finished with 29 points.

Led by Malone and Hornacek, the Jazz overcame a 36-point deficit. Utah's amazing second half stunned the Nuggets. Utah outscored the Nuggets 71–33 after halftime to claim the 107–103 victory. Through 2016–17, it was still the largest deficit ever overcome in an NBA game.

"When you are 34 points ahead, you're basically obligated to go on and win," Denver head coach Dick Motta said. On most nights in NBA history, a lead that big would have been good enough. On this night, however, it was not.

LeBron James dunks over Harrison Barnes in the NBA Finals.

CAVS DOWN, BUT NOT OUT

Sometimes a remarkable comeback happens in a few seconds. Sometimes it happens over a quarter or two. Sometimes the remarkable comeback takes a few games. That was the case for the Cleveland Cavaliers in the 2016 NBA Finals.

The Golden State Warriors were the defending world champions. They were favored to win it again. That season, they set an NBA record for wins, going 73–9. They also had the league's two-time MVP, Stephen Curry.

Four games into the NBA Finals, the Warriors led the Cleveland Cavaliers three games to one. None of the games had been particularly close. Golden State won Game 1 by 15 points and Game 2 by 33 points. Cleveland won Game 3 by 30 points. But in Game 4, the Warriors won by 11.

The Cavaliers would need to win three straight games to survive and win the title. No team had ever done that in the Finals. After the first four games, Cleveland didn't appear to be the team to do it.

The Cavaliers, however, weren't giving up. With star forward LeBron James leading the way, they didn't think about winning three games. "Let's get one," James said after Game 4.

Getting that one wouldn't be easy. Games 5 and 7 would be played on the Warriors' home floor at Oracle Arena. The Warriors were 50–3 at home during the regular season and playoffs. To win the championship, Cleveland had to figure out how to win two games at Oracle Arena.

But the Warriors' tough forward Draymond Green had been suspended for one game. Cleveland took advantage. James scored 41 points, grabbed 16 rebounds, and passed out seven assists. Guard Kyrie Irving also scored 41 points. That all added up to a 112–97 win, pulling Cleveland one game closer.

The Cavaliers still needed two wins and had no room for error. Game 6 was back in Cleveland. Energized by the home crowd, the Cavs led 31–11 after the first quarter. They never looked back in a 115–101 victory. James again had 41 points for the Cavs. It was on to do-or-die Game 7 in California.

With 5:25 to play in Game 7, the Warriors led by four. James scored six points in 35 seconds, including a three-pointer, to take

LeBron James chases down Andre Iguodala to block his shot.

HOMETOWN HERO

LeBron James was born in Akron, Ohio, and the Cleveland Cavaliers were his hometown team. He spent seven seasons with the Cavs before leaving for Miami. James played in Miami for four seasons, winning two championships with the Heat. He returned to the Cavs in 2014 and promised a championship. He delivered in 2016.

the lead. Warriors guard Klay Thompson tied the game at 89–89 with 4:39 left.

It was still 89–89 with just under two minutes to play. The Warriors went on a fast break, with Andre Iguodala going up for a layup. From behind, James came flying in and swatted the ball away for a huge block.

Nearly a minute later, Irving launched a three-pointer over Curry and drained it. The Cavs had pulled off a stunner, 93–89. James had 27 points, 11 rebounds, and 11 assists in the game, and played great defense. He was named the MVP of the Finals.

The Cavaliers won their first NBA championship. It was the first major professional sports championship by any Cleveland team in 52 years.

HONORABLE MENTIONS

ROCKETS 81, SPURS 80: In December 2004, Tracy McGrady scored 13 points in just 33 seconds of the fourth quarter. McGrady scored 33 points in the game to lead the Rockets to an improbable 81–80 win over a dominant San Antonio Spurs team.

LAKERS 105, MAVERICKS 103: The Lakers were down 30 at the beginning of the third quarter in December 2002. They rallied behind Kobe Bryant and Shaquille O'Neal. Bryant scored 21 of his 27 points in the fourth quarter including a shot with 8.4 seconds left to beat Dallas 105–103.

CLIPPERS 99, GRIZZLIES 98: In the 2012 playoffs, the Clippers trailed the Memphis Grizzlies by 27 with just over two minutes left in the third quarter. Behind excellent players from the bench, Los Angeles rallied to win. It was the second-largest comeback in playoff history.

TRAIL BLAZERS 84, MAVERICKS 82: The Trailblazers overcame a 23-point deficit in Game 5 of the first round of the 2011 playoffs to beat the Dallas Mavericks. Behind LaMarcus Aldridge and Brandon Roy, Portland outscored Dallas by 20 points in the fourth quarter to win 84–82.

WARRIORS 112, RAPTORS 103: The Warriors were down by 27 to Toronto at the beginning of the third quarter. It was an early season game in December 2013. Stephen Curry drained 27 points to power the comeback on the Warriors' home court. Golden State came all the way back to win 112–103.

MAVERICKS 107, TIMBERWOLVES 100: The Dallas Mavericks trailed the Minnesota Timberwolves in December 2008 by 29 points in the third quarter. They rallied behind Dirk Nowitzki and Jason Terry, who combined for 53 points, to win 107–100.

GLOSSARY

ASSIST
a pass that leads directly to a basket.

COMEBACK
when a team losing a game rallies to tie the score or take the lead.

MOMENTUM
the sense that a team is playing well and will be difficult to stop.

OVERTIME
an extra period of play when the score is tied after regulation.

PLAYOFFS
a set of games played after the regular season that decides which team is the champion.

REBOUND
to catch the ball after a shot has been missed.

SWEEP
winning every game in a series.

THREE-POINTER
any shot taken behind the three-point line.

TRIPLE-DOUBLE
accumulating 10 or more of three certain statistics in a game.

UPSET
an unexpected victory by a supposedly weaker team or player.

MORE INFORMATION

ONLINE RESOURCES

To learn more about the NBA's greatest comebacks, visit
abdobooklinks.com. These links are routinely monitored and updated to
provide the most current information available.

BOOKS

Borth, Teddy. *Basketball: Great Moments, Records, and Facts*. Minneapolis,
   MN: Abdo Publishing, 2015.

Graves, Will. *Basketball Record Breakers*. Minneapolis, MN: Abdo
   Publishing, 2016.

Silverman, Drew. *Basketball*. Minneapolis, MN: Abdo Publishing, 2012.

PLACE TO VISIT

NAISMITH MEMORIAL BASKETBALL HALL OF FAME
1000 Hall of Fame Avenue
Springfield, MA 01105
877–446–6752
hoophall.com

The Basketball Hall of Fame is like a museum dedicated to basketball.
It highlights the greatest players, coaches, and moments in the sport's
history. Many of the players mentioned in this book are enshrined there. It
is home to more than 300 inductees and more than 40,000 square feet of
basketball history.

INDEX

ABOUT THE AUTHOR

Brian Howell is a freelance writer based in Denver, Colorado. He has been a sports journalist for more than 20 years and has written dozens of books about sports and two about American history. A native of Colorado, he lives with his wife and four children in his home state.